EXPLORING THE SUBATOMIC WORLD

Understanding
NEUTRINOS

B. H. Fields
and Fred Bortz

Cavendish Square
New York

To my classmate, friend, and world-class neutrino-catcher, Professor Lawrence R. Sulak

Published in 2016 by Cavendish Square Publishing, LLC
243 5th Avenue, Suite 136, New York, NY 10016

Website: cavendishsq.com

This publication represents the opinions and views of the author based on his or her personal experience, knowledge, and research. The information in this book serves as a general guide only. The author and publisher have used their best efforts in preparing this book and disclaim liability rising directly or indirectly from the use and application of this book.

CPSIA Compliance Information: Batch #WS15CSQ

All websites were available and accurate when this book was sent to press.

Library of Congress Cataloging-in-Publication Data

Fields, B. H.
Understanding neutrinos / by B. H. Fields and Fred Bortz.
p. cm. — (Exploring the subatomic world)
Includes index.
ISBN 978-1-50260-540-5 (hardcover) ISBN 978-1-50260-541-2 (ebook)
1. Neutrinos — Juvenile literature. 2. Particles (Nuclear physics) — Juvenile literature. I. Fields, B. H. II. Title.
QC793.5.N42 F48 2016
539.7'215—d23

Editorial Director: David McNamara
Editor: Andrew Coddington
Copy Editor: Cynthia Roby
Art Director: Jeffrey Talbot
Designer: Stephanie Flecha
Senior Production Manager: Jennifer Ryder-Talbot
Production Editor: Renni Johnson
Photo Research: J8 Media

The photographs in this book are used by permission and through the courtesy of: DeAgostini/Getty Images, cover; maralova/Shutterstock.com, throughout; By Loon, J. van (Johannes), ca. 1611–1686. (http://nla.gov.au/nla.map-nk10241) Public domain, via Wikimedia Commons, 7; Dr. Long's copy of Cassini/File:Cassini apparent.jpg/Wikimedia Commons, 8; Nicku/Shutterstock.com, 9; Thomas Forget, 10; Paul Nadar, Public domain/File:Portrait of Antoine-Henri Becquerel.jpg via Wikimedia Commons, 15; SSPL/Getty Images, 17; By Bain News Service, publisher,Public domain/File:Ernest Rutherford 1908.jpg via Wikimedia Commons, 20; Thomas Forget, 22, 23; Encyclopaedia Britannica/UIG/Getty Images, 24; Science & Society Picture Library/Getty Images, 26; Ann Ronan Pictures/Print Collector/Getty Images, 29; Thomas Forget, 30, 33; Fermi National Accelerator Laboratory/Science Source/Getty Images, 35; Max-Planck Institute, courtesy AIP Emilio Segre Visual Archives, 36; Jiu/Imaginechina/AP Images, 38; Research Laboratory of Electronics/Greg Hren Photography, 41; Thomas Forget, 42; Science Source, 45; AIP Emilio Segre Visual Archives, 48; Thomas Forget, 50; Courtesy of the SNO+ Collaboration, 51; Thomas Forget, 52; NASA, ESA, M.J. Jee and H. Ford (Johns Hopkins University) File:CL0024+17.jpg/Wikimedia Commons, 54.

Printed in the United States of America

Contents

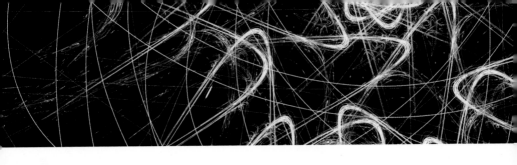

Introduction

This is the story of a kind of subatomic particle that you have probably never heard about. Yet it is more numerous by far than the ones you probably know. It is called the **neutrino**, Italian for "little neutral one." Neutrinos speed through space, pass through matter, and rarely leave a trace. Still, on the rare occasions that we dectect them, they tell a remarkable story.

That story begins with facts you probably have learned in school. Every substance is made of **atoms**, and atoms are made of smaller subatomic particles called **protons**, **neutrons**, and **electrons**. Protons and neutrons carry most of the atom's mass and make up its central region, called the **nucleus**. Electrons are much lighter. You may have been told that the electrons orbit the nucleus like planets orbit the sun. That's a useful way to view an atom, but, as you will discover, it is not exactly correct. And that is only the beginning of the story.

Besides those three kinds of subatomic particles, there are many others that are not found in matter as you are used to thinking about it. The neutrino is one of those other particles. In the chapters ahead, you will discover that neutrinos carry no electric charge, have very little mass, and are very hard to detect. Yet understanding neutrinos is essential to make sense of the entire subatomic world.

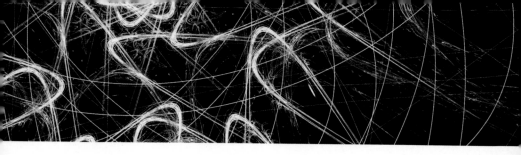

Although neutrinos are not contained within atoms, they are created within them. They come out of a nucleus during one kind of radioactive decay. They also emerge when heavy subatomic particles transform into lighter ones, or when nuclei merge together in a process called **fusion**. Fusion fuels the stars. Stars not only produce light and heat, but they also send vast numbers of neutrinos streaming outward.

Billions of neutrinos zip through your body every second without affecting it at all. In fact most neutrinos that reach Earth pass through without interacting with even a single atom. It takes careful scientific work to detect those few that do. In fact, it took about twenty-five years from the time physicists (scientists who study matter and energy) first realized that neutrinos were necessary in nature's "scheme of things" until a team of researchers identified them in a nuclear reactor.

To understand neutrinos, you first need to understand atoms and their parts, especially the nucleus and the phenomenon of **radioactivity**. The nucleus was discovered little more than a century ago, and physicists are still exploring the forces within it. This book follows the path of discovery from the nucleus to the modern limits of particle **physics**—where nearly massless, uncharged, barely detectable sprites known as neutrinos turn out to reveal the deepest secrets of the universe.

1 MATTER
and the Forces of Nature

Physics is a mathematical science. When people hear or read that, they immediately think about equations or formulas. Those formulas often arise from patterns that physicists see in natural phenomena. Then they look for fundamental principles underlying those patterns.

The process often goes like this: At first, a pattern seems complex. Then someone discovers a new viewpoint from which things appears to be simpler. That viewpoint often leads to important discoveries about the laws that govern nature. Although this book will eventually take you to unfamiliar forces deep within atoms, it begins with a force you experience all the time: gravity.

The Universe According to Ptolemy. The second-century Greek-born Egyptian mathematician and astronomer Ptolemy observed and described the motion of the Sun, Moon, stars, and planets in several important texts. It was natural, though incorrect, for people of that time to view Earth as the center of all motion, as shown in this illustration based on Ptolemy's writings.

Patterns of Planetary Motion

To people of ancient civilizations, Earth was unmoving and the center of everything. The Sun, Moon, and stars seemed to have followed regular paths around it, day after day, year after year. Everything in the heavens followed easily predicted paths—except for the planets. People recorded their motions across the sky and discovered that they would sometimes speed up, sometimes slow down, and sometimes even reverse their direction of movement.

The paths of planets across the sky weren't as predictable as the motion of the Sun, Moon, and stars. So the sky-watchers had to do a little tinkering with the natural laws to make planetary motion fit. They began with a simple modification:

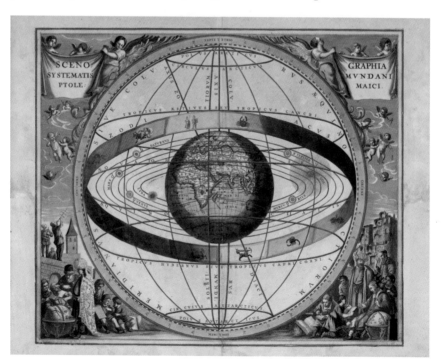

Suppose each planet's path consisted of a small circle called an epicycle whose center moved around Earth's circumference in a larger circle. That matched observations fairly well, but as they gathered more detailed measurements, the epicycles failed to match the planets' movements. Soon they began adding epicycles to epicycles and things were beginning to look too complicated to be sensible.

Some people found a different way of interpreting planetary motion, with the Sun at the center of the solar system and Earth and all the other planets in orbit around it. That got rid of many epicycles, but not all. For more than a thousand

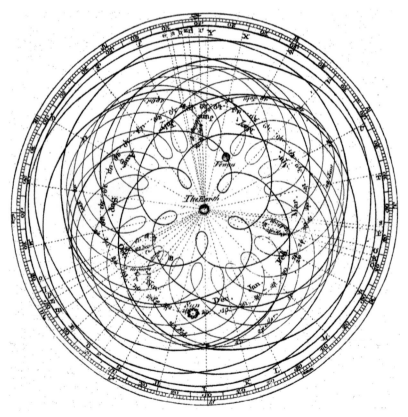

Epicycles. The observed movements of the planets could not be explained by simple circular paths around Earth, so Ptolemy added epicycles—circular paths around a point moving on a larger circle—to explain it. That resulted in diagrams like this one.

Nicolaus Copernicus (1473–1543). As measurements of the motion of planets became more precise, astronomers began to realize that the Earth-centered view of planetary motion was incorrect. An alternate view, with the sun as the center of all motion, gave a better explanation. Copernicus adopted that idea and wrote a book that persuaded many people that Earth was a planet like the others.

years, most people were reluctant to accept that their world was not the center of everything. Finally, Polish astronomer Nicolaus Copernicus (1473–1543) wrote a book that persuaded many people that Earth was a planet like the others.

Copernicus's idea finally took hold when German astronomer Johannes Kepler (1571–1630) applied his mathematical talents to the best astronomical measurements of his time. He found that the planets moved not in circles, but in curved paths called ellipses. He also discovered two other mathematical formulas that described the details of the motions of planets in their orbits. Thanks to Kepler, nature was once again governed by simple laws. Still, those laws were

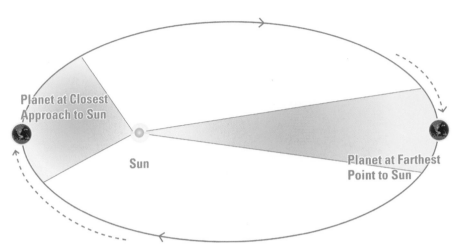

Kepler's First Two Laws. Johannes Kepler's observations of the planets led him to propose three mathematical laws to describe their orbits. The first states that a planet's orbit around the sun is not a perfect circle but rather a more elongated shape called an ellipse. Instead of having one center like a circle, an ellipse has two points called foci (plural of focus). The Sun is at one focus. His second law notes that the speed of a planet changes along its path in a particular way. The result is that the line from the sun to the planet sweeps out the same area over any given time interval.

only a description of planetary motion, not an explanation of the underlying cause.

That explanation came from Sir Isaac Newton (1642–1727): he proposed that the laws of nature are the same everywhere. The same gravitational force that attracts apples downward from trees also draws the Moon toward Earth and the planets toward the Sun. Newton also developed three laws of motion that scientists and engineers still rely on today. The first two laws describe how an object's motion changes when a force acts on it. The third law states that any interaction between two bodies consists of equal forces acting in opposite directions on them.

Newton expressed those laws as mathematical formulas and used them to analyze the motion of a smaller body orbiting a much larger one, such as the planets rotating around the Sun. Out popped elliptical orbits and Kepler's other two formulas. Thanks to Newton, gravity was recognized as a universal force. His third law of motion also established an important principle that would lead to the discovery of the neutrino centuries later. Because the forces on two interacting bodies are equal and opposite, so are their changes in momentum (a quantity that measures the direction and intensity of motion). Thus the total momentum before, during, and after the interaction remains unchanged. That principle, known as conservation of momentum, has been a pillar of physics for more than three centuries.

Principles and Patterns of Chemistry

In the nineteenth century, scientists studied other forces that might also be universal, particularly electricity and magnetism, which were discovered to be different aspects of the same phenomenon called electromagnetism. Meanwhile, English meteorologist John Dalton (1766–1844) had begun studying the gases of the air, hoping his research would help him to understand more about weather. He ended up transforming the science of chemistry instead, by reviving an ancient idea that all substances were made of indivisible bits called atoms. In his 1810 book titled *A New System of Chemical Philosophy*, Dalton wrote about **elements**, substances made of only one kind of atom, and **compounds**, substances made of specific combinations of atoms called **molecules**.

Dalton observed chemical reactions to determine how different elements combine with each other and to calculate their atomic masses. He set the **atomic mass** of hydrogen, the lightest element, at one unit, and based the mass of other atoms on that. Dalton also stated an important principle about the way matter could change in chemical reactions. The atoms might reshuffle in their combinations, but they never changed from one element to another. As a result, the mass before the reaction was the same as the mass afterward, a principle known as conservation of mass.

As chemists identified more compounds and the elements that composed them, they gradually developed a list of the atomic masses and other properties of each element. By the end of the 1860s, scientists knew of sixty-three elements and could see distinct similarities and differences among their properties. They could group elements according to patterns in their atomic masses, their melting or boiling points, their densities (the mass of each cubic centimeter), the way they combined with other elements, and the properties of the compounds they formed. Still, no one had come up with a successful arrangement of the elements that would enable people to see all these similarities and differences on a chart. Such a chart might also reveal an underlying principle of matter.

Early in 1869, Dmitri Ivanovich Mendeleyev (1834–1907), a chemistry professor at St. Petersburg University in Russia, was taking a long train trip. While en route, he occupied himself by arranging and rearranging a deck of homemade cards, each listing an element and its properties, as if playing solitaire. He finally discovered a pattern that made sense. Starting from the smallest atomic mass and increasing as he went along, he laid out a column of cards. He continued until he came to an element that had the same chemical property called "valence" as one of his earlier cards. Then he would start a new column and repeat the process, producing rows of elements with the same valence.

An element's valence describes how it tends to form compounds with other elements. For example, the alkali metals (lithium, sodium, potassium, rubidium, and cesium) all form compounds of one atom each with nonmetallic elements known as halogens (fluorine, chlorine, bromine, and iodine). The alkali metals have a valence of +1 and the halogens have a valence of −1, so the compound has a net zero valence. Valence also relates to electrical properties of the elements, as chemists were discovering by passing electricity through compounds dissolved in water.

Because the patterns of similar valence repeated, Mendeleyev called his arrangement the "periodic table of the elements." It is still in use today, though with the elements in rows and the valences in columns. The arrangement had gaps, but that was the most important part of Mendeleyev's success. He recognized that the gaps represented undiscovered elements. He boldly predicted not only which elements would be found, but also what their atomic masses and densities would be. Later discoveries showed that his predictions were true!

The periodic table provided powerful evidence that atoms, though not yet observed directly, were real. But why was it periodic and how was that related to valence? It took the more than sixty years of research to find the explanation, and part of it was because Dalton was not quite correct. He was right that atoms are the smallest bits of an element, but he was wrong to consider them indivisible.

Particles Within the Atom

As the nineteenth century was ending, two major discoveries provided hints that atoms were made of smaller pieces. The first was the phenomenon of radioactivity, and the second came from the study of cathode rays. In February 1896, French physicist Antoine Henri Becquerel (1852–1908) was studying substances that glow in the dark after being exposed to sunlight, such as compounds of the rare metal uranium. He soon discovered that they produced radiation even without being exposed to sunlight.

In the next few years, chemists and physicists discovered a number of radioactive elements, and laboratories all around the world began to study the nature of radioactivity. By then, physicists had developed another important principle, conservation of energy, to go along with conservation of mass and momentum. Energy might change form, such as from the heat of steam to the mechanical motion of a piston, but it could not be created or destroyed. Radioactivity seemed to violate that principle, but physicists viewed it in another way. Energy had to be conserved, so some other form of energy was being converted into radioactive energy. But what was it? Radioactivity was sending physicists down a path to new discoveries.

In 1895, just as the news about X-rays sent physicists scurrying to learn more, a promising young student from New Zealand, Ernest Rutherford (1871–1937) arrived at the Cavendish Laboratory of Cambridge University in England. Lab director J. J. Thomson (1856–1940) promptly assigned Rutherford the task of understanding the newly discovered X-rays, and then extended the assignment to include radioactivity when Becquerel announced his surprising results.

Meanwhile, Thomson was busy with the final stages of a series of experiments to understand the cathode rays seen in glass tubes from which most of the air had been removed. The terminals of a battery or electric generator were connected to two electrodes in that tube. The cathode, or negative electrode, was a heated metal filament. It emitted a beam, called a cathode ray, that caused a glow. Thomson's objective

Antoine Henri Becquerel (1852–1908). Becquerel's discovery of radioactivity in 1896 led physicists to consider that atoms might be made of smaller particles.

was to find out what that beam consisted of, and in 1897, he announced his results.

Cathode rays were tiny particles less than a thousandth as massive as a hydrogen atom. Yet it carries as much negative electricity as the hydrogen atom does in positive charge.

Thomson's Cathode Ray Experiments

J. J. Thomson's cathode ray tubes were made of glass with most of the air pumped out. Two electrodes, one positive (the anode) and one negative (the cathode), were inserted at opposite ends. When electricity was applied, the remaining gas would glow, especially near the cathode. Scientists who first experimented with such tubes called that glow cathode rays. They knew that the cathode was shooting out tiny, negatively charged particles. But they were divided about whether the particles themselves were the cathode rays, or whether the glow resulted from waves that the particles produced. Thomson hoped to settle the question by performing various experiments.

Thomson applied magnetic fields to the tubes, and the rays curved in the direction that the magnetic field would cause negatively charged particles to curve. But when he passed the beam between a pair of oppositely charged electrified plates, the cathode rays went straight through, producing a glowing spot on the center of the glass. If cathode rays were streams of negative particles, the glowing spot on the glass should have been offset in the direction of the positively charged plate—but it wasn't.

Puzzled, Thomson put a device that measures electrical charge into the tube. When struck by the glow, the device indicated a large negative charge. When the glow just missed, it measured very little charge. From that, Thomson concluded that cathode rays were either a stream of negative charges or they carried such a stream with them. But why did the results with the electrified plates seem to show an uncharged stream?

Thomson reasoned that an energetic beam of negative particles would electrify the gas it passed through, and the charged gas atoms would drift toward the oppositely charged plate, neutralizing the electric field within the tube. If he could do a better job of removing the gas from the tube, there would be too few molecules to neutralize the electric field. He got the best available vacuum pump and tried the experiment again. Sure enough, the cathode rays now deflected toward the positive plate. Thomson was now confident that they were negatively charged "corpuscles," that is, particles, shot from the cathode.

Additional experiments allowed Thomson to measure the ratio of the particles' electric charge to their mass. To his astonishment, he discovered that each corpuscle had less than a thousandth of the mass of the tiny hydrogen atom.

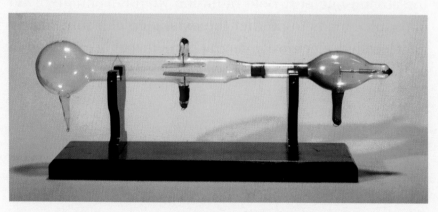

Thomson's Cathode Ray Apparatus. J. J. Thomson used the best available vacuum pumps to remove the air from this glass tube. The heated cathode (*right*) created cathode rays that deflected as they passed through the pair of electrically charged plates. Thomson eventually realized that the cathode rays were tiny, negatively charged subatomic particles that we now call electrons.

Today, we know more precisely that this particle's mass is only $\frac{1}{1,837.15}$ of the hydrogen atom. Thomson called the particles "corpuscles" and concluded that they were particles from within the atoms of the metal. That meant the atom was not indivisible. Today we know those first subatomic particles as electrons, and we know that they are responsible for the chemical behavior of every substance.

Might radioactivity also come from inside atoms? Rutherford began to answer that question in his three years at the Cavendish Laboratory, where he discovered that radioactivity had two distinct forms, which he named alpha and beta radiation after the first two letters of the Greek alphabet. He discovered that, like Thomson's corpuscles, alpha and beta radiation were electrically charged particles coming from within the atom. He continued to study them when he became a professor at McGill University in Montreal, Canada, in 1898.

Each of those forms of radiation is important to our story. Alpha radiation would lead Rutherford to discover the atomic nucleus. Beta radiation would eventually lead other physicists to predict the existence of a tiny, nearly undetectable, electrically neutral particle that became known as the neutrino.

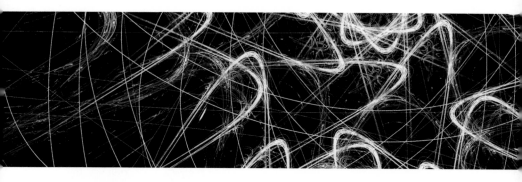

2 NEUTRINOS
Save the Day

Rutherford's first experiments with radioactivity at the Cavendish Laboratory measured how far it could penetrate matter. He quickly recognized two different types of radioactivity, which he called alpha and **beta rays**. Alpha rays could be easily stopped by a few layers of aluminum foil, but beta rays penetrated much more deeply.

Physicists around the world quickly recognized the importance of his discovery. In 1898, he accepted an offer of a professorship at McGill University in Montreal, Canada, which had one of the world's best physics laboratories. By 1900, he had discovered a third even more penetrating form of radiation, which he called **gamma rays**. Rutherford also found hints that radioactivity violated one of Dalton's fundamental principles by transforming one element into another. For example, radioactive thorium was producing an "emanation," a radioactive gas, which we now know as the element radon.

Ernest Rutherford (1871–1937) in 1908. Not long after returning to England, Rutherford was awarded the Nobel Prize in Chemistry for his work on the chemistry of radioactive substances. But an even more important discovery lay ahead: the atomic nucleus in 1911.

Rutherford needed a chemist to analyze the changes and found the perfect colleague in Frederick Soddy (1877–1956), who had just arrived at McGill. Together, Rutherford and Soddy tracked the elements from their original form to their new forms. They found that when an atom emits an alpha ray, its atomic mass decreases by four units and its atomic number (its position in the periodic table) decreases by two. When it emits a **beta particle**, its atomic number increases by one unit, but its atomic mass doesn't change. They recognized that this wasn't a chemical reaction but a **transmutation**, the transformation of an atom of a "parent" element into the atom of a different element, a "daughter" element. The daughter is frequently more radioactive than its parent, so there is a continuing sequence of transmutations—a chain of alpha or beta decays—from one atom to another to another.

A Nuclear Surprise

Rutherford and Soddy were clearly on the track of something important. Becquerel had already identified beta rays as light, negatively charged particles—electrons, in fact. Rutherford and Soddy found that alpha rays were also particles, but much heavier than beta rays and carrying positive electric charges. Transmutation results suggested that an **alpha particle** was a helium atom without its electrons. Today we call that a helium nucleus, but the atomic nucleus was still to be discovered—by Rutherford. That great discovery took place back in England at the University of Manchester, where Rutherford accepted a professorship in 1907.

At Manchester, Rutherford used alpha particles as bullets, directing a beam of them at thin metal foils. If he could measure their **scattering**, or the pattern of their deflections,

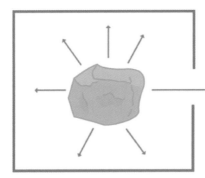

Radioactive Source

Rutherford's Scattering Experiment. With students Hans Geiger and Ernest Marsden, Rutherford set out to determine the internal structure of an atom by scattering alpha particles from a metal foil. Most of the alpha particles passed through with little or no change in direction, but a few bounced back toward the radioactive source. This astonishing result led Rutherford to the idea of a heavy but very small nucleus at the heart of an atom, surrounded by orbiting electrons.

from the atoms in the foil, that might reveal the atoms' size, spacing, and perhaps even their shape or internal structure. J. J. Thomson had proposed that atoms were like plum pudding, with the atomic number of electrons scattered like tiny plums in the pudding's positively charged bulk. Other scientists thought they were more like little hard balls. Rutherford's scattering experiments showed that neither idea was right.

To perform those experiments, Rutherford needed an instrument to detect and count the scattered alpha particles. His student Hans Geiger (1882–1945) devised that instrument (which came to be called a Geiger counter) in 1909 and began the scattering experiments. Nearly all the alphas passed straight through the foil or deflected only slightly. That fit with J. J. Thomson's plum pudding model, which had nearly all the mass and enough positive electric charge spread out to balance the negative electrons.

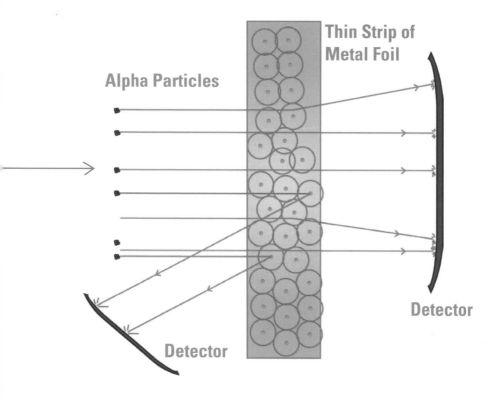

Alpha Particles

Thin Strip of Metal Foil

Detector

Detector

But Geiger's experiments also produced a puzzle. His detectors were very accurate, and even though he had them spread out over a large angle, a small but significant fraction of the alpha particles were unaccounted for. Had they scattered beyond the detectors? If so, what could cause such scattering through such large angles? Rutherford thought the task of looking for large-angle scattering would be good experience for Ernest Marsden (1889–1970), a young student just learning the techniques of research. Marsden found the missing alpha particles. Some went to the left or right of the original detectors, and a few even scattered backward. Rutherford described this result as "almost as incredible as if you had fired a 15-inch (38-centimeter) shell at a piece of tissue paper and it came back and hit you."

By 1911, Rutherford had an explanation for the results. Atoms, he stated, were like miniature solar systems, mostly empty space and held together by electricity instead of gravity. Tiny electrons are the planets, carrying only a small fraction of the system's mass. The central body, called the nucleus, though much more massive, is very compact, occupying about one ten-thousandth of the diameter of the atom. The emptiness of the atom explains why most alpha particles pass through with little scattering. But on those rare occasions when a fast-moving alpha particle makes a nearly direct hit on a heavy nucleus, the alpha scatters sideways or even backward.

Rutherford then set out to understand what made one element's nucleus different from another. In 1919, he replaced the retiring J. J. Thomson as leader of the Cavendish Laboratory at Cambridge University. By then, physicists accepted Rutherford's idea that the nuclei contain a number

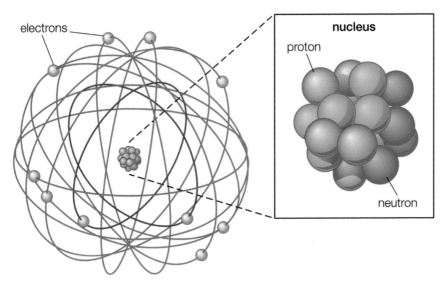

The Atom According to Rutherford. Having discovered the nucleus, Rutherford went on to determine what made an atom of one element different from an atom of another. He proposed that nuclei are made up of two types of particles with about the same mass: protons, which carry a positive electric charge; and neutrons, which are electrically neutral. Orbiting the nucleus are the atom's electrons.

of protons, particles that carry the same amount of positive electric charge as the electron's negative charge. They also agreed that the atomic number of an element was the number of electrons it had in its electrically neutral state—which is the same as the number of protons in its nucleus. Thus the nucleus of hydrogen was a single proton and alpha particles were helium nuclei with two units of positive electrical charge and an atomic mass of four. From where did the extra atomic mass units come?

For larger atoms, the discrepancy between atomic number and atomic mass was even greater. Lead, for instance has atomic number 82 and atomic mass 207. Rutherford proposed that the extra mass came from electrically neutral subatomic particles with about the same mass as protons. He called them neutrons. Alpha particles, for example, consisted of two protons, each with one unit of positive electric charge, and two uncharged neutrons.

A New Physics Emerges

Rutherford had correctly explained that alpha decay occurs when a stable helium nucleus bursts out of a larger unstable nucleus. His explanation of beta emission, however, was not quite correct. He said that it resulted from the splitting of a neutron in an unstable nucleus, producing a proton and an electron. That seemed sensible, until physicists studying the energy of beta particles ran into problems with conservation laws.

The early decades of the twentieth century were full of major surprises for physicists. Probably the most famous of these was the theory of relativity, devised in 1905 by Albert

Chadwick and the Neutron

Not all physicists agreed with Rutherford's idea that nuclei contained neutrons. Some insisted that an atomic nucleus had more protons than the atomic number enough electrons to reduce the electric charge. They all agreed that detecting uncharged particles would be difficult because that had no electric charge. The argument continued until 1932, when James Chadwick (1891–1974), one of Rutherford's colleagues at the Cavendish Laboratory, figured out a way to detect neutrons indirectly but convincingly.

Chadwick's Neutron Chamber. James Chadwick (*right*) used this chamber in 1932 to repeat experiments by Irene Joliot-Curie and Frederic Joliot that produced neutral beams. He showed that the beams were streams of particles with masses similar to protons, matching the properties of Rutherford's predicted neutrons.

Chadwick built on the reasearch of two German scientists, Walther Bothe (1891–1957) and Herbert Becker. In 1930, they discovered that bombarding beryllium metal with a beam of alpha particles produced a powerful outward going beam of neutral radiation. Wondering whether that beam was gamma rays, Irene Curie (1897–1956), the daughter of the famous Pierre and Marie Curie, and her husband Frederic Joliot (1900–1958), directed that neutral radiation at paraffin wax, which is rich in hydrogen, and found that it was knocking out protons. Gamma rays could shake electrons loose from matter, but they had never been observed to eject heavier particles such as protons.

When Chadwick heard of that result, he was certain that the neutral beam was composed of neutrons. He did a series of experiments in which he allowed the beam to collide with a variety of gases. By measuring the scattering of the nuclei of those gas atoms, he was able to measure the mass of the particles in the beam, which turned out to be almost exactly the same mass as a proton. That confirmed Rutherford's description of the makeup of atoms: compact nuclei in the center composed of protons and neutrons that carried most of their mass, surrounded by lightweight electrons.

Einstein (1879–1955). One of its most surprising predictions—even to Einstein himself—was that mass and energy are two aspects of the same phenomenon, as represented by the formula $E = mc^2$. The amount of energy in a unit of mass can be determined by multiplying the mass by the speed of light (c) times itself (or squared). That formula explains the source of the energy carried off by alpha or beta rays. As scientists made careful measurements of the mass of parent and daughter nuclei in radioactive decay, they discovered that the mass of the daughter element plus the emitted alpha or beta particle was less than the mass of the parent. When that missing mass was put into Einstein's formula, the result matched the emitted alpha particle's kinetic energy (energy of motion). For all alpha decays from a particular parent nucleus, the alpha particle always carried off the same amount of energy.

For beta emission, the results were less satisfying. The beta particles from a parent nucleus had a range of kinetic energies, from very little to a maximum amount that fit Einstein's equation. Where was the missing energy of the slower beta particles?

An additional puzzle about beta decay arose from a newly developed description of the subatomic world. Called **quantum mechanics**, it had revealed that a particle like an electron is described by a set of properties that can only have certain values—or **quantum numbers**. Collectively these properties are called its quantum state.

One of these properties describes its magnetic alignment by a quantity called **spin**. Spin, like energy and momentum and electric charge, is conserved in any interaction of particles. For protons, neutrons, and electrons, the spin values are the same (½ of a natural quantity known as Planck's constant), but they may have either a positive or negative sign. Beta

Albert Einstein in His "Miracle Year," 1905. Einstein burst to fame among his fellow physicists with a series of groundbreaking publications in 1905, including one that related mass and energy by the formula $E = mc^2$.

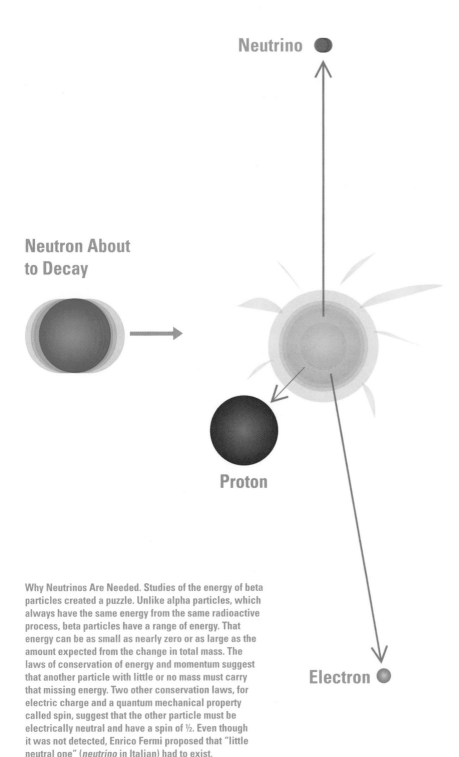

Neutrino ●

Neutron About to Decay

Proton

Electron ●

Why Neutrinos Are Needed. Studies of the energy of beta particles created a puzzle. Unlike alpha particles, which always have the same energy from the same radioactive process, beta particles have a range of energy. That energy can be as small as nearly zero or as large as the amount expected from the change in total mass. The laws of conservation of energy and momentum suggest that another particle with little or no mass must carry that missing energy. Two other conservation laws, for electric charge and a quantum mechanical property called spin, suggest that the other particle must be electrically neutral and have a spin of ½. Even though it was not detected, Enrico Fermi proposed that "little neutral one" (*neutrino* in Italian) had to exist.

emission begins with a neutron, so the total spin before decay is either +½ or −½. If the only products of the emission are a proton and an electron, the total spin afterward is +1, −1, or zero. The total electric charge is zero before and after beta emission. But what can be done to give the same total spin after the emission as before?

In 1930, Austrian physicist Wolfgang Pauli (1900–1958) suggested that the beta particle must be emitted with a partner. That partner would have a spin of ½, but it would be electrically neutral and have little or no mass. In 1933, physicist Enrico Fermi (1901–1954) developed a theory of beta decay that incorporated what he called the "little neutral one," or neutrino in his native Italian. Its lack of charge and low mass would make it very hard to detect, but all signs pointed to its existence. Finally, in 1956, using measurements made inside a nuclear reactor where there were lots of neutrinos flying around, physicists managed to detect a few.

The discovery of the neutrino saved the theory of beta decay. That turned out not to be the only heroic feat of this tiny electrically neutral sprite. Nearly fifty years later, neutrinos seemed to be performing a disappearing act. But what they were really doing was revealing something fundamental about the subatomic world.

3 NEUTRINO
Number Two and the Particle "Zoo"

The new field of quantum mechanics was about more than quantum numbers. It also led to a new scientific understanding of the nature of matter and energy. It seems natural to think of particles as made of matter with definite places, shapes, and sizes, and waves as carriers of energy spread out and moving in space and time. But at the subatomic level, quantum mechanics tells us that waves and particles are two aspects of the same thing.

Consider, for example, electrons in atoms. In Rutherford's planetary model of the atom, electrons orbit the nucleus like planets moving around the sun. In quantum mechanics, electrons are like tiny vibrating violin strings with their ends tied together to make that orbital shape. Likewise, quantum mechanics describes light and other electromagnetic energy as flowing not in perfectly smooth waves but rather as grainy streams of particles that we now call **photons**.

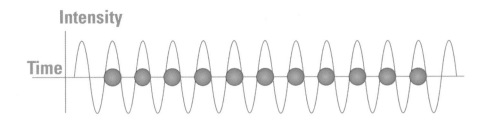

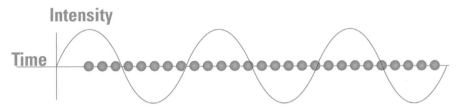

Grainy Waves of Light. Quantum mechanics developed from a surprising discovery that light can behave as both a wave and a grainy stream of particles called photons. As shown here, the energy of a photon is larger when the frequency of light is higher. That discovery required a new way of viewing the laws of electromagnetism called Quantum Electrodynamics (QED), which describes electric attraction or repulsions as a result of charged particles exchanging photons.

Though blending waves and particles seemed as odd as discovering that mass and energy are the same thing, physicists quickly accepted both quantum mechanics and relativity because those theories were extraordinarily successful in describing a wide variety of atomic and subatomic phenomena. Light really is grainy, electrons really can act like waves, and the energy of radioactivity comes from transforming some mass.

But that means some very successful older theories of physics, such as the equations of electromagnetism that produced smooth electromagnetic waves, need to be modified at the subatomic level. Many physicists struggled to come up with a new description of electromagnetism, which they called **quantum electrodynamics,** or QED for short. Although QED was not fully developed until the 1940s, physicists made a good start on it in the 1930s when they described electromagnetic forces between electrically charged particles as the result of exchanging photons between them. If the particles had opposite electric charges, the photon exchange produced an attraction. If they had the same charge, the photon exchange would lead to repulsion (pushing apart). In QED, the photon is the carrier of the electromagnetic force.

Naturally, physicists wondered if a different exchange of particles might explain how the nucleus holds together despite having all those electrically repelling protons clustered in such a small space. Could protons and neutrons be exchanging particles too? In 1935, Japanese physicist Hideki Yukawa (1907–1981) developed a theory suggesting that nuclei hold themselves together by a force we now call the **strong nuclear force**, or simply the **strong force**. It results from exchanging particles known as **pions**, each with a mass about 250 times that of an electron. Another force within the nucleus, the **weak nuclear force** (or simply the **weak force**), explains beta decay, because it keeps a neutron from transforming into a proton, electron, and neutrino most—but not all—of the time.

Pions, Muons, and the Subatomic "Zoo"

Could physicists detect those pions and confirm Yukawa's bold prediction? The tools for detecting subatomic particles were improving, and scientists began looking for pions in cosmic rays, the stream of high-energy particles striking Earth from space. Another possible source of pions was in powerful new machines that could accelerate particles to very high energies.

In 1937, scientists discovered particles in cosmic ray particles that had about the expected mass of a pion. But they turned out to be quite different. They did not respond to the strong force. Instead, they seemed to be super-sized electrons,

From Cosmic Rays to Accelerators. Although muons were first detected in cosmic rays, they are now frequently produced in giant machines called particle accelerators. This photograph shows the Central Detector at Fermilab (Fermi National Accelerator Laboratory) near Chicago, Illinois, including two muon chambers in the foreground.

particles that we now call muons. "Who ordered that?" asked famous physicist Isadore Isaac Rabi (1898–1988), wondering where muons fit in the subatomic world.

With improved detectors, in 1947 cosmic ray physicists finally found pions and their super-sized cousins kaons in cosmic rays. That was only the beginning of the story. By the end of the 1950s, an entire "zoo" of subatomic particles

Real Forces from Virtual Particles

An odd feature of Quantum Electrodynamics is the way it includes "virtual" particles. Those particles are the result of the uncertainty principle of quantum mechanics, which was first described by Werner Heisenberg (1901–1976). Because particles have wavelike properties, it is impossible to measure their position or energy exactly. The more precisely you try to measure a particle's position, the less precisely you are able to measure its speed. Likewise, to measure a particle's energy, you need to take a certain amount of time. The uncertainty principle states that the uncertainty in energy

multiplied by the length of time of your measurement has to be at least Planck's constant. This means that "virtual" particles can pop in and out of existence without violating the law of conservation of energy as long as they only last a short period of time.

As long as that length of time multiplied by the particles' energy is less than Planck's constant, the uncertainty principle permits them. Quantum electrodynamics is based on the appearance and disappearance of virtual photons. It seems like an odd theory because of that, but it matches experimental results so well that physicists consider it to be a valid description of nature.

Yukawa's theory of the strong nuclear force is based on the exchange of virtual pions. Unlike massless photons, the pions' energy is in the form of their mass. And because they have mass, they can't travel at the speed of light. That means they can't travel beyond the limits of the nucleus during their short existence. Yukawa's theory matched observations so well that physicists expected to find real pions outside a nucleus when they add enough energy to it. With that extra energy, the pions no longer needed to be virtual. In 1947, that's exactly what cosmic ray physicists found.

Werner Heisenberg's Mathematics. Heisenberg's approach to quantum mechanics led to the principle of uncertainty. That led to the idea of "virtual" particles, which appear from nowhere and disappear a very short time later. Though that seems odd, the exchange of virtual particles underpins two very successful ideas: Yukawa's theory of the strong nuclear force, and quantum electrodynamics.

Murray Gell-Mann (1929–). Gell-Mann, shown here after a 2010 lecture at Huazhong Normal University in Wuhan, China, is often considered a twentieth-century Mendeleyev for his 1961 discovery of a way to arrange subatomic particles according to their properties, bringing order to the particle "zoo."

with names like lambda, sigma, and xi had been discovered in cosmic rays and particle accelerators. In 1962, they even found a second neutrino, which they named the muon neutrino because it appeared to be a partner to the muon in the same way that the renamed electron neutrino was to the electron.

As the number of subatomic particles grew, physicists were faced with a question similar to the one chemists struggled with a century earlier as more elements were discovered. They noticed hints of patterns in the properties of these new particles, but they couldn't figure how to classify them. That problem was solved by Murray Gell-Mann (1929–).

In 1954, Gell-Mann and Japanese physicist Kazuhiko Nishijima noticed that the interactions of these new particles seemed to be obeying conservation laws not only for known quantities (such as energy, charge, spin) but also for a quantity that had no clear physical significance. Gell-Mann called that quantity "strangeness." In 1961, Gell-Mann and amateur physicist Yuval Ne'eman (1925–2006), a colonel in the Israeli army, each recognized that these particles had properties that fit a certain mathematical pattern.

The symmetries in this pattern, which Gell-Mann called the Eightfold Way—because it had groupings of eight particles—suggested the existence of a particle that had not yet been discovered. (The name was inspired by the Noble Eightfold Path of Buddhism.) Gell-Mann described that particle's properties, including its negative charge. Because it would complete the pattern, he named it the omega-minus after the last letter of the Greek alphabet. It was discovered in 1964, confirming Gell-Mann's hypothesis.

Unlike Mendeleyev, who recognized the periodicity of the elements but did not know the underlying principles, Gell-Mann was able to devise a theory about what lay behind the

George Zweig's Aces

As is often the case in science, breakthrough ideas sometimes come from more than one person at the same time. Murray Gell-Mann was not the only physicist to consider the possibility that protons, neutrons, and strange particles were not fundamental. In 1964, the same year that Gell-Mann first described **quarks**, George Zweig (1937–) wrote about a similar model of the subatomic world.

Zweig's theory was based on four particles instead of Gell-Mann's three. Because there are four suits in a deck of cards, he called his proposed fundamental units aces. His "spade" work was quite valuable in shaping scientific thought about the "heart" of matter. His ideas proved more than exceptional, and many important scientists believe that he deserves a place in the Nobel Prize "club."

Zweig has received significant recognition for his scientific work, first in physics, and later in neurobiology, where he specialized in understanding how structures within the human ear translate sound into nerve impulses that reach the brain's auditory cortex.

Quarks or Aces? Great ideas often spring from more than one person when the time is right. George Zweig came up with the idea of smaller particles making up protons, neutrons, and strange particles at about the same time as Gell-Mann. He proposed that there were four such particles (matching the electron, the muon, and the two neutrinos known at that time) and called them aces. Gell-Mann's theory was more successful, so his chosen term, quarks, trumped Zweig's aces.

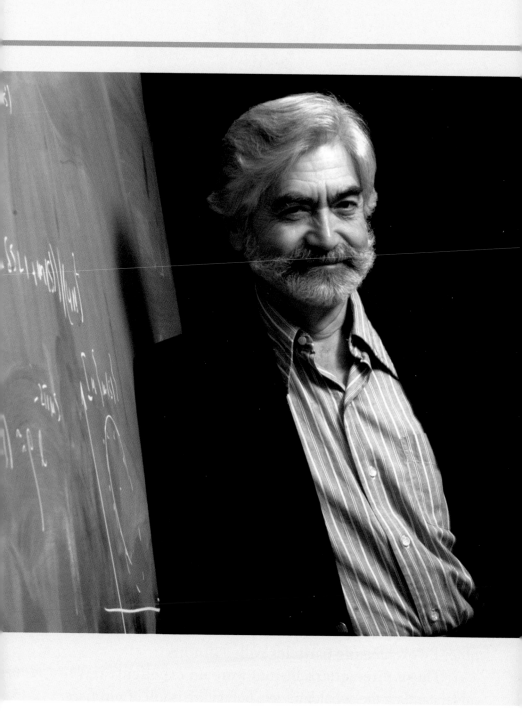

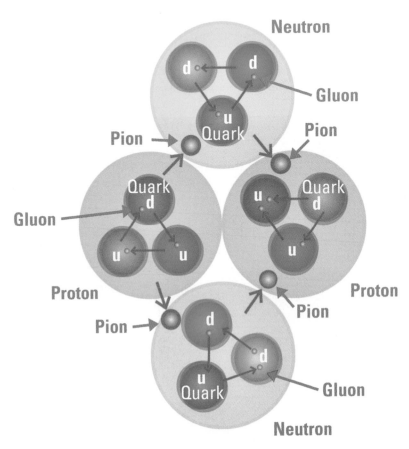

The Strong Nuclear Force at Work. This diagram shows how the exchange of pions holds a helium nucleus (or alpha particle) together. Each proton and neutron consists of three quarks, one of each "color." The protons and neutrons attract each other by exchanging pions, which are made of a quark and an antiquark of the corresponding anticolor. Within the protons and neutrons, the quarks bind together by exchanging gluons.

pattern. Just as atoms are made of smaller parts, he realized that protons, neutrons, and strange particles are also not fundamental particles. Rather, they are composed of three smaller entities that he named quarks. The strong force is not only between protons and neutrons, but also between the quarks that compose them. He described three quark "flavors," which he called up, down, and strange, that interact with each other by exchanging particles called **gluons**.

Those three quark flavors were an excellent start to understanding the subatomic zoo, but nature is full of surprises.

Other physicists discovered a way to combine electromagnetism and the weak force into what became known as the electroweak force. For that to work, nature need to have another quark, which they called "charm."

By 1974, the list of basic subatomic particles consisted of four quarks, the electron and the muon plus their corresponding neutrinos, and the particles that carried the electroweak and strong forces. During the following year, the tau—a more massive version of the electron and the muon—came along. And with it came the prediction of two more quarks and another neutrino.

It seemed as if another subatomic zoo might be on the way, populated with a series of generations of foursomes. Each foursome would have its electron-like particle with a different Greek letter for a name, a neutrino-like partner to that electron-like entity, plus pairs of quarks. How many generations might there be? Would there be enough Greek letters for the electron-like particles and clever names for the quarks? Neutrinos detected in the deep underground provided the surprising answer, and that is the subject of the closing chapter of our story.

4 A UNIVERSE
of Neutrinos

Although the first members of the particle zoo (except for protons, neutrons, and electrons) were discovered in cosmic rays, by the mid-1950s, scientists were using particle accelerators, large machines sometimes familiarly called atom smashers, to look for other undiscovered particles. Those machines accelerate protons, electrons, and other subatomic particles—and most recently large nuclei—to high velocities and enormous kinetic energy. They smash those particles into targets or make them collide with other particles, causing some of their energy to be transformed into mass.

That mass takes the form of various particles in the zoo. Charged particles are much easier to detect than neutral ones. As they pass through matter, they knock loose electrons from atoms, and produce a trail of electrically charged ions that can be detected in a number of ways. For example, if they pass through a vapor just on the edge of condensing into a liquid, a streak of cloud condenses on the ions. That effect is similar to the way high-flying airplanes produce streaks in the sky. Cloud chambers, used as early as the 1890s for studying the **ionization** due to X-rays and radioactivity, were the earliest devices used to detect particles in cosmic rays around 1910.

Many other particle detection techniques have since been developed. They employ strong magnetic fields, so charged particles passing through them follow circular arcs. Positive charges curve in one direction and negative charges curve in the opposite. The radius of the curve enables the experimenters to determine the particle's momentum.

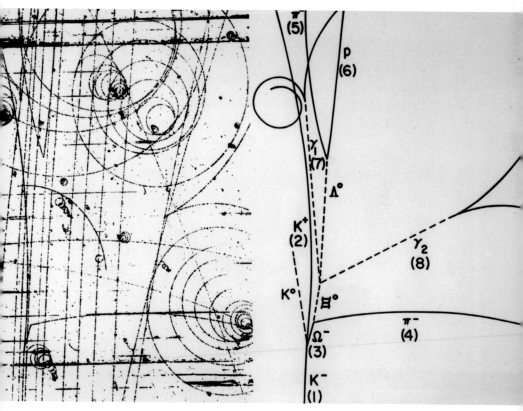

Cloud Chamber Image and Interpretation. Just as planes leave contrails in the sky, subatomic particles produce tracks as they pass through a cloud chamber. This image shows the detection of the omega-minus particle that confirmed Gell-Mann's prediction of the Eightfold Way.

The First Particle Accelerator

Studying subatomic particles in cosmic rays is difficult because scientists can't control what comes from space or predict where and when they should look. By the early 1930s, physicists wanted to create intense, controllable particle beams for their experiments. In 1931, Ernest Orlando Lawrence (1901–1958), a physics professor at the University of California at Berkeley, built the first particle accelerator for that purpose. He called his device the cyclotron, and many of the great particle accelerators in use today are based on Lawrence's original ideas.

Lawrence's goal was to build a machine powerful enough to accelerate alpha particles and give them sufficient energy to free Yukawa's predicted pions from nuclei. He was finally able to achieve that energy with technological advances made during World War II. Lawrence's cyclotron design is based on a pancake-shaped vacuum chamber separated by a gap into two D-shaped regions or "dees." The particles to be accelerated enter the chamber near its center at one side of the gap. An alternating-current (AC) source creates a large electric field across the gap that reverses direction at the same rate as the source switches. In effect, the gap is a powerful battery that accelerates the particles from one of the dees to the other.

A magnetic field causes the particles to follow a semicircular path around that dee. When the particles reach the gap again, the electric field has reversed, and that further accelerates the particles. They now follow a slightly larger semicircle around the other dee. That process repeats, speeding up the particles with each crossing of the gap until they reach the outer edge and emerge at very high speed toward their target. How fast is that speed?

Suppose there were 1,000 volts across the gap and the particles make five hundred complete circles, or one thousand gap crossings. The particles would then reach the speed created by a one million–volt battery!

Lawrence in his Laboratory. Ernest Orlando Lawrence, inventor of the cyclotron, is shown here at the controls of one of his later models, which featured a chamber 27 inches (68.6 centimeters) in diameter.

If they can determine its energy (which they often can from characteristics of the trail or other knowledge), that gives them the particle's mass. Knowing mass and charge is usually enough to identify exactly which member of the particle zoo the detector has caught. It may also indicate the discovery of a previously unknown particle.

Beyond Muons and Charm

Thanks to particle accelerartors and advanced detectors, physicists could do more than just discover subatomic particles. They could also study the relationships between those particles. Physicists frequently witnessed events in which one particle would transform into lighter ones, converting the lost mass into energy of the outgoing particles. By measuring energy and momentum of electrically charged particles before and the transformation, they might deduce that an unseen neutral particle had been produced.

Sometimes that neutral particle would reveal itself by colliding with a charged particle or by transforming itself into a pair of oppositely charged particles. It sounds complex, and it is. Particle physicists (and their computers) have to plow through enormous amounts of data to catch a glimpse of rare subatomic particles and events. That mass of information explains why in 1974, while they were celebrating the discovery of the first particles known to contain charm quarks, they hadn't quite noticed the hints of another surprise in their experiments. The discovery of the charm quark seemed to tie up many loose ends. Matter was apparently built from four quarks, which responded to the strong nuclear force, and four **leptons** (the electron, the muon, and their matching neutrinos) that did not.

In 1975, physicists once again had to ask, "Who ordered that?" A new lepton appeared in their experiments. It behaved in the same way as the tiny electron and the heavier muon, but its mass was nearly four thousand times as great as the electron. They called it the tau particle, and they presumed that it, like the muon, would have a matching neutrino as well. That seemed to call for two more quarks, named top and bottom (or more colorfully, truth and beauty). Between 1995 and 2000, particle physicists found evidence of both new quarks and the tau neutrino, but they couldn't help wondering if other generations of particles remained to be discovered.

By 2002, much to the surprise of many, nature was providing hints that the there were no more generations to be found. To read those hints, scientists had to gather neutrinos from sunbeams. Physicists detect subatomic particles by the way they interact with matter through electromagnetic and nuclear forces. The three types of neutrino carry no electric charge, so they don't interact electromagnetically. And, as leptons, they don't interact through the strong force. The weak force, to which neutrinos will respond, keeps particles like neutrons together, but not perfectly. The most likely way to detect a neutrino would be in a rare process of reverse beta decay, in which the weak force between a very energetic neutrino and a proton produces a neutron and a positively charged version of the electron called a positron.

To catch a neutrino in this way would require either a lot of energetic neutrinos or a lot of protons. In 1956, two physicists at Los Alamos Scientific Laboratory set out to perform the hardest experiment they could think of: neutrino detection. Nuclear reactors produce lots of neutrinos, so they built a detector that could operate in that intense environment. They detected the neutrinos indirectly from flashes of light

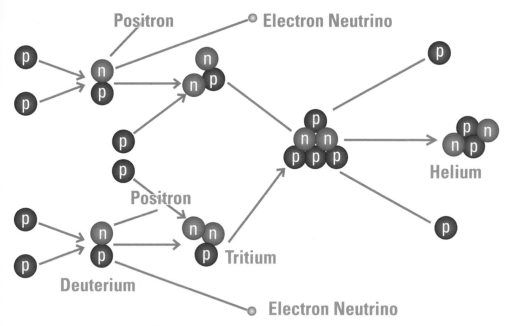

The Solar Neutrino Factory. Our Sun, just like other similar stars, produces its energy through the process of nuclear fusion, or the combining of smaller nuclei into larger ones. Most of that energy comes from combining hydrogen nuclei (protons) in a multi-step sequence that leads to helium nuclei. In the first step of that process, two protons join to form a deuterium nucleus (heavy hydrogen, with one proton and one neutron), a positron, and an electron neutrino.

produced by the positrons in a detector, confirming that neutrinos really exist. Meanwhile, astrophysicists had been developing theories about the way the sun and other stars produce their energy by a process called nuclear fusion. In that process, light nuclei (like hydrogen) combine to form heavier ones (like helium), with some mass being transformed into energy. The theories were quite successful in explaining the behavior of the stars and the mixture of different atoms in the universe. They also predicted the number of neutrinos streaming from the Sun to Earth every second.

Neutrinos from the Sun are more spread out than neutrinos from a nuclear reactor. So to test the theory, scientists needed a detector that would respond to a reverse beta decay, plus lots of protons to catch the neutrinos. Cosmic rays might produce similar signals in their detectors, so the device had to be placed far underground where neutrinos were the only particles that would penetrate. The first such device was a large vat of cleaning fluid—the molecules of that liquid has lots of hydrogen atoms—surrounded by instrumentation. It went into operation in the Homestake Gold Mine in South Dakota in the 1980s. This was just in time to detect neutrinos from a giant supernova explosion in a neighboring galaxy in 1987. But it wasn't long before scientists noticed a problem.

Scientists knew how many solar neutrinos to expect, but the instruments were detecting far too few. Larger neutrino detectors were build in Japan and Canada, and they, too, found

The Sudbury Neutrino Observatory (SNO). Even though neutrinos are very tiny, they interact so rarely with other matter that scientists need huge detectors to spot them. The detectors must be deep underground so that other subatomic particles such as cosmic rays do not reach them. This 59-foot- (18-meter-) diameter sphere is in a cave more than a mile underground in Canada. (Note how small the people appear in this picture.)

too few solar neutrinos—only about one-third the expected number. Was something wrong with the theory of the sun's nuclear fusion? Was something wrong with the detector? Or was something wrong with the theories about neutrinos and their interactions with matter?

Particle theorists had an unusual suggestion. Their equations were telling them that the three different kinds of neutrino might not be different after all. As a neutrino moves

Neutrinos Lost in Space? Physicists studying the Sun were able to predict the number of solar neutrinos that their detectors should capture, but the results were showing only one-third as many. The other two-thirds seemed to be lost on the way to Earth. Particle theorists had an explanation they called neutrino oscillation. The detectors were only capturing electron neutrinos, but the theory suggested that neutrinos could change from electron neutrinos to muon and tau neutrinos as they travel. By the time solar neutrinos reach Earth, the three types are evenly mixed. The Sudbury Neutrino Observatory could—and did—detect all three types, solving the mystery.

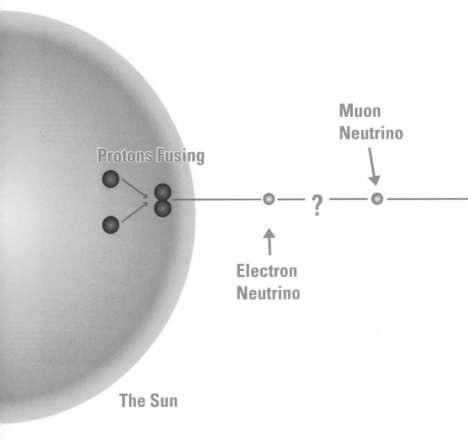

Muon Neutrino

Protons Fusing

Electron Neutrino

The Sun

through space, it might repeatedly change from an electron neutrino to a muon neutrino to a tau neutrino. This process is referred to as oscillation. After the long trip from the Sun, the neutrinos would arrive as an even mix of all three types. In 2002, experimenters at the Sudbury Neutrino Observatory, in a nickel mine deep beneath Ontario, Canada, were able to detect all three types of neutrinos. Oscillation, they discovered, was indeed taking place.

One way to describe their result is to say that there is only one type of neutrino with three different modes. Since the older solar neutrino detectors only picked up neutrinos in their electron mode, they would only register a third of the expected number. The measurements matched the theory after all. If matter had a fourth set of basic subatomic particles, then the neutrino would have four modes and even fewer would be detected. So the Sudbury result points to a limit to the number of new generations of subatomic particles.

Earth

Neutrinos may also offer clues to other cosmic mysteries that have emerged in the late twentieth and early twenty-first centuries. For instance, cosmologists—scientists who study the history of the universe—are puzzled about missing mass, which they call dark matter, that seems to exist in and between galaxies. Galaxies and galaxy clusters spin so fast that they would fly apart if they only experienced the gravity

Dark Neutrinos? One of astronomy's greatest mysteries is dark matter. The rotation of galaxies and galaxy clusters shows that they must contain much more mass than the total of all their visible stars. Without the gravity of that missing mass, they would spin themselves apart. This composite image from the Hubble Space Telescope shows a dark ring produced by a phenomenon called gravitational lensing, in which a massive object distorts the light from more distant sources behind it. The ring itself is not dark matter but it may be evidence of dark matter left over after the collision between two massive galaxy clusters. If so, it may help answer the question of whether some or all of the universe's dark matter is comprised of so-called sterile neutrinos.

of their visible members. Might some of that missing mass come from neutrinos? Perhaps.

One theory is that besides the electron-, mu-, and tau-neutrinos, there is a fourth type scientists call "sterile" because it does not respond to the weak nuclear force and thus would not be seen in current neutrino detectors. The neutrino, that little neutral particle that first rescued the principles of conservation of momentum and energy in beta decay and later ended the search for new generations of quarks and leptons, is full of surprises. Who knows what other discoveries await as we continue along the path to understanding neutrinos!

Glossary

alpha particle A helium nucleus that is emitted from some radioactive elements.

atom The smallest bit of matter than can be identified as a certain chemical element.

atomic mass The mass of an atom of a chemical element expressed in atomic mass units. For naturally occurring elements, it is approximately equal to the number of protons plus the average number of neutrons in the nuclei.

beta particle or **beta ray** An electron that is emitted from some radioactive elements.

compound A substance made of only one kind of molecule that consists of more than one kind of atom. For example, water is made of molecules that contain two atoms of hydrogen and one atom of oxygen.

electron A very light subatomic particle (the first to be discovered) that carries a negative charge and is responsible for chemical properties of matter.

element A substance made of only one kind of atom.

fusion A process in which lighter nuclei combine to form heavier nuclei and release energy. This process powers the stars and produces neutrinos that stream outward into space.

gamma ray A high-energy photon that is emitted from some radioactive elements.

gluon A particle that is exchanged between quarks, resulting in their being bound together.

ionization A process in which neutral atoms are turned into electrically charged ions by gaining or losing electrons.

lepton A subatomic particle that does not respond to the strong nuclear force. The leptons include electrons, muons, taus, and their corresponding neutrinos.

molecule The smallest bit of matter that can be identified as a certain chemical compound.

neutrino A subatomic particle with very little mass and no electric charge that is emitted along with an electron in beta radiation.

neutron A subatomic particle with neutral electric charge found in the nucleus of atoms.

nucleus The very tiny, positively charged central part of an atom that carries most of its mass.

photon A particle that carries electromagnetic energy, such as light energy.

physics The science of matter and energy.

pion A subatomic particle that carries the strong nuclear force, binding protons and neutrons together in the nucleus.

proton A subatomic particle with a positive electric charge found in the nucleus of atoms.

quantum electrodynamics (QED) A mathematical description of the electromagnetic force that accounts for quantum mechanical phenomena.

quantum mechanics A field of physics, developed to describe the relationships between matter and energy, that accounts for the dual wave-particle nature of both.

quantum number One of several numbers that specifies the state of a property of a subatomic particle, such as its orbital characteristics within an atom or its spin.

quark A sub-subatomic particle that exists in several forms that combine to make protons, neutrons, and some other subatomic particles.

radioactivity A property of unstable atoms that causes them to emit alpha, beta, or gamma rays.

scattering An experimental technique used to detect the shape or properties of an unseen object by observing how other objects deflect from it.

spin A property of subatomic particles expressed by a quantum number, also called spin, that describes the way it may align in a magnetic field.

strong nuclear force or **strong force** A fundamental force of nature that acts to hold the protons and neutrons in a nucleus together.

transmutation A transformation of the nucleus of one element into another by emission of an alpha or beta particle.

weak nuclear force, or **weak force** A fundamental force of nature that is responsible for beta decay of a radioactive nucleus.

For Further Information

Books

Bortz, Fred. *The Periodic Table of Elements and Dmitry Mendeleyev*. New York: Rosen, 2014.

Bortz, Fred. *Physics: Decade by Decade. Twentieth-Century Science*. New York: Facts On File, 2007.

Green, Dan, and Simon Basher. *Extreme Physics*. New York: Kingfisher, 2013.

Hagler, Gina. *Discovering Quantum Mechanics*. New York: Rosen, 2015.

Marsico, Katie. *Key Discoveries in Physical Science*. Minneapolis, MN: Lerner Publications, 2015.

Morgan, Sally. *From Greek Atoms to Quarks: Discovering Atoms*. New York: Heinemann Publishing, 2008.

Marsico, Katie. *Key Discoveries in Physical Science.* Minneapolis: Lerner Publications, 2015.

Morgan, Sally. *From Greek Atoms to Quarks: Discovering Atoms.* New York: Heinemann Publishing, 2008.

Websites

American Institute of Physics Center for the History of Physics
www.aip.org/history-programs/physics-history

This site includes several valuable online exhibits from the history of physics, including The Discovery of the Electron and Rutherford's Nuclear World.

The Nobel Foundation Prizes for Physics
www.nobelprize.org/nobel_prizes/physics

Read about past Nobel Prize winners associated with the neutrino, Ernest Rutherford, Louis de Broglie, Albert Einstein, Murray Gell-Mann, and others.

The Science Museum (UK)
www.sciencemuseum.org.uk

This site includes the online exhibit Atomic Firsts, which tells the story of J. J. Thomson, Ernest Rutherford, and Thomson's son George Paget Thomson, who also won the Nobel Prize for his experiment that proved the existence of de Broglie's predicted electron waves.

Museums and Institutes

American Chemical Society (ACS)
1155 Sixteenth Street NW
Washington, DC 20036
(800) 227-5558
portal.acs.org/portal/acs/corg/content

Chartered by the US Congress, the ACS is one of the world's leading sources of trustworthy and accurate scientific information.

American Institute of Physics
Center for the History of Physics
One Physics Ellipse
College Park, MD 20740
(301) 209-3165
www.aip.org/history-programs/physics-history

The Center for History of Physics houses a research library, a photo archive, and has created numerous online resources in all areas of physics, including Rutherford's Nuclear World.

Ernest Rutherford Collection
Room 111 Ernest Rutherford Physics Building
McGill University
3600 rue University
Montréal, QC H3A 2T8
Canada
(514) 398-6490
www.mcgill.ca/historicalcollections/departmental/ernest-rutherford

On permanent display at the Rutherford Museum is the apparatus used by Nobel Prize winner Ernest Rutherford when he was professor of experimental physics at McGill from 1898 to 1907.

Lederman Science Education Center
Fermilab MS 777
Box 500
Batavia, IL 60510
(630) 840-8258
ed.fnal.gov/lsc/lscvideo/index.shtml

Visit the Lederman Science Education Center and explore the science and history of subatomic particles.

Ontario Science Centre
770 Don Mills Road
Toronto, ON M3C 1T3
Canada
(416) 696-1000
www.ontariosciencecentre.ca

The Ontario Science Centre is Canada's leading science and technology museum. Its programs and exhibits aim to inspire a lifelong journey of curiosity, discovery, and action to create a better future for the planet.

Index

About the Authors

Science educator and consultant **B. H. Fields** has worked behind the scenes in the publishing industry since the mid-1980s, specializing in books and articles on the physical sciences and technology for middle grades.

Award-winning children's author **Fred Bortz** spent the first twenty-five years of his working career as a physicist, gaining experience in fields as varied as nuclear reactor design, automobile engine control systems, and science education. He earned his PhD at Carnegie Mellon University, where he also worked in several research groups from 1979 through 1994. He has been a full-time writer since 1996.